HOW TO WRITE FANTASY NOVELS

VOLUME I: GETTING STARTED

ADAM STEMPLE

Copyright © 2021 by Adam Stemple

All rights reserved.

No part of this book may be reproduced in any form or by any electronic or mechanical means, including information storage and retrieval systems, without written permission from the author, except for the use of brief quotations in a book review.

❦ Created with Vellum

For JY,
who taught me everything in this book and more besides

INTRODUCTION

About Me

I GREW UP READING AND writing fantasy. My mother is a Science Fiction & Fantasy Writers of America (SFWA) Grandmaster, and though I didn't appreciate getting my nine-year-old journals back edited in red pen, it paid off in the end. As of this writing, nine fantasy novels that I have written or co-written have been traditionally published, and I have self-published a tenth. My co-author and I won the Locus Award for Best Young Adult Fantasy in 2006, and Anne McCaffrey called my first solo novel, an urban fantasy entitled *Singer of Souls*, "One of the best first novels I've ever read." I have written and sold historical fantasy, epic fantasy, urban fantasy for the YA, middle grade, and adult markets. I have talked, taught, and lectured on fantasy at conventions and conferences for decades. I decided it was finally time to write down all I've learned over the years. I believe it will be of use to people who wish to write fantasy.

Why Fantasy?

THAT'S A GOOD QUESTION TO ask yourself, because it's going to affect what and how you write. For me, I began writing fantasy because as a child reader there was nothing I liked better than being lifted completely out of this world and brought to another. Epic fantasy was my jam—in a series if possible, and the more books, the better. I read Tolkien, Lloyd Alexander, Patricia McKillip and more. Then I discovered Emma Bull, Meghan Lindholm, Charles DeLint and other urban fantasy pioneers. Suddenly, you could twist the real world and make it as magical as Middle Earth or the Island of Hed. Glen Cook's *The Black Company* let me know how dark fantasy could get—at least until Grimdark became a genre. And then there were the works that were definitely fantasy, but defied additional descriptors.

When I began writing professionally, it was no surprise that I wrote primarily fantasy. It was also unsurprising that I covered a lot of sub-genres, too. If you prefer to specialize, that's fine. What's important is that you are widely read in the genre you intend to write in. You need to know what has already been done in that genre. You need to know what the tropes and clichés are. Not that you need to avoid reworking an old idea or adhere to the conventions of others, but it's important to know these things so you can approach them with your eyes open.

A Warning

OF ALL THE WRITING ADVICE I've read or received—and there's been plenty—the best piece came from my first agent, the wonderful Marilyn Marlow. I was talking to her on the phone about the struggles I was having in writing my first solo novel. After listening to my travails, she said simply, "You're just learning how you write."

Not how *to* write. How *you* write.

I thought about that with every new "How To" book on writing I read. I found that the books that told you how *to* write were next to worthless. They outlined a system, a program, a step-by-step process for how to write. In my experience, no matter the genre or style of the book you're trying to write, there is no one system that can teach you how to do it. And anyone who tells you that there is, is just trying to sell you something.

And yet, here I am writing a book that will purportedly tell you how to write fantasy novels. Let me explain.

The books on writing that I found the most helpful were the ones where the author outlined what worked for them, without presenting them as The One True Way to Write. It was all about *their* method. *Their* tricks. *Their* tools. They knew that there was no one way to write, no one way to edit, no one way to be successful. So they merely wrote what worked for them, and allowed me to pick and choose the pieces that fit with my style of writing. Or better yet, they explained what they were trying to accomplish with their particular methods so that even if their way didn't work, I could devise another way to get the same result.

That is what I attempt to do in this series of books: detail the tools I use to create fantasy books and encourage you, the reader, to adopt them or devise your own, so that by the end of the series, you are a capable and confident fantasy author, ready to create the magical worlds and compelling characters that make readers love fantasy books so much.

1

THE BASICS

Before we can talk about writing fantasy, there are some basic writing fundamentals we have to discuss. I will try to get through them as swiftly as possible, but they can't be ignored.

Grammar is important

Before you can write fantasy, you have to make sure you can write. If you can't construct a decent sentence, no amount of clever world-building is going to result in a decent book. Though you don't have to follow the rules of grammar—most writers break them with wild abandon—you have to know them. And more importantly, you have to know why they're there.

To my mind, the best way to do that is to go to the source: Strunk & White's *Elements of Style*. It's old, but still contains the best and most concise explanations for the rules of grammar and why they matter. But of course, any book on grammar that resonates with you and allows you to learn will work. Because you really need to know the rules. Why?

So you can break them.

See, I broke one just now. *Because you really need to know the rules* isn't a sentence; it's a sentence fragment. But one of things that *Elements of Style* teaches is that mixing up the length of your sentences breaks up the monotony of the prose and helps the reader stay engaged. I like to go the extra mile and break even sentences down into smaller pieces. So, whilst I break one of the basic blocks of grammar, I do it in the service of a greater grammarly cause: reader engagement.

The rules of grammar are intended to make reading easy. To let the story flow into the reader without unnecessary distractions. To allow the reader to be transported away from the world and into the world of the story they're reading—which in fantasy, is of utmost importance. You're going to be asking the reader to believe a lot of crazy stuff. Make sure your words aren't getting in the way of that belief.

And, of course, this last rule can also be broken. See Anthony Burgess's *A Clockwork Orange* where the language is a near impossible barrier at the start of the story and essential to engagement by the end, or Steven Brust's *The Phoenix Guards* where the verbose garrulity of the narrator is *most* of the story.

Still, I can guarantee that both authors broke the rules intentionally and for very specific reasons.

How to tell if you can write

. . .

THE PROBLEM WITH WRITING IS that everyone who speaks a language thinks they can write it, as well. And no one is less qualified to judge the quality of a piece of prose than the person who wrote it. Ask any writer, and most will tell you that their perception of their own work vacillates wildly from "this is a work of staggering and heartrending genius" to "I am the worst writer in all of history" depending on what day they happen to read it. As authors, we're too close to it. You can develop a good editing eye for your own work, but only after you've taken a whole lot of critiques. My suggestion, join a writers group.

I prefer a small group. For me, I find that knowledge of who is critiquing your work is as important as the critique itself. Are they a fantasy reader? Do they know the tropes? Did a Midwestern author of popular urban fantasy books beat up their mom and now I've just handed them a dark tale of elves in modern-day Topeka? These are not things I will know if I submit to a large online site with anonymous reviewers.

But that might work for you. The anonymity might help you get over the fear of being critiqued. You might get a much wider range of people reviewing your work. You might even get some fans if people are particularly entranced by your prose. Like I said in the warning, I can only tell you what works for me. However you do it, try to get eyes on your work that can give you an honest read and accurately detail any problems they see in it.

People will tell you that you have to have a thick skin to be a writer. And you do. Critiques hurt, but they are the pain of excising the errors from your document, the missteps from your storyline, the false traits from your characters. This is almost always a painful process. But with good critiquers, it is less so.

A good critiquer…

- *Starts with something positive about the story.* We have a joke in my writers group that if a reader starts their critique with "I really liked the font you picked for this story," then you know you're in for a rough ride.
- *Doesn't let personal preference affect their critique.* The stuff I write is often darker and more violent than the other writers in my group prefer. But they are able to put their personal taste aside and critique my work without prejudice.
- *Are specific with their problems and vague with their solutions.* A critiquer's job is to spot the problem; it's your job to fix it.
- *Don't take their problems out on you.* Writing is a frustrating business. That means there are a lot of frustrated writers out there, and some of them delight in tearing down other writers to make themselves feel better. If there's a bully in your group, kick them out or go join a new group.

Look for these traits in people and train them in yourself. You don't want to be the person who is always taking and never giving. Besides, you'll find you often learn more about writing by critiquing others than you do by writing yourself.

Critiques are great, but…

. . .

THERE'S NOTHING WRONG WITH having friends who simply love your work uncritically. People you can count on to be a cheerleader and keep your spirits up when the writing is hard. Because sometimes, you just need someone to tell you you're awesome, not to point out every detail that's wrong in your work in progress.

Dare to Suck

MY FRIEND AND OFTTIMES engineer, Leo Whitebird, has spoken these words to me through my headphones before many a music track I've recorded with him. I utter them to myself now whenever I write. Don't worry about writing something good, just get it down. Worry about putting something awful down on paper has ruined more good writers than rejections or reviews. Dare to suck. You can make it suck less when you revise.

All right, that's enough basics. Time to get started!

2

FOUR ELEMENTS TO GET STARTED

Every author I know has a story about a friend or relative telling them, "I have this great idea for a novel. You should write it and we can split the money."

This is the biggest misconception about writing, that the idea is the important part. Frankly, the idea is the easy part. People who don't write always get this wrong. Either they think they have this great idea and just need to get someone to write it up for them, or they think they can't write because they don't have that one million-dollar idea. Neither is true. If you have an idea, it's on you to write it up. Don't try to foist that thing off on us. Most writers have a thousand ideas of their own that they won't get to in their lifetime; they certainly aren't looking to add someone else's idea to the list.

And if you're not writing because you haven't yet found the perfect concept for your world-shattering debut fantasy novel? Stop. Or rather, start. Once you let go of the idea that you need to wait for that one brilliant idea to begin, then you can *actually* begin.

Besides, this so-called "idea" is merely a collection of these four elements that you can start a novel from. You can start with one, some, or all of them in mind, but by the end, your book will contain all of them. That means you can build your idea from the slimmest of beginnings. You don't need to know everything about your book before you begin. That's what rewriting is for.

I will return often to these elements no matter what part of the process we're in, as they are the building blocks of not just fantasy, but of writing itself.

The elements are setting, characters, plot, and theme.

Setting

IN FANTASY NOVELS, ESPECIALLY secondary world fantasy, setting is *everything*. You are introducing the readers to an entirely new world, a world of your own imagination. It is a delicate task, and any missteps can erode their trust in you. I do a lot of world-building, in my urban fantasy as well as epic. I want my fantasy world to be as complex and nuanced as the real world so the reader has no excuse to ever think, "No, that's just not real."

Suspension of disbelief is a delicate thing; care must be taken to ensure your reader keeps believing in your world.

Characters

IF SETTING IS EVERYTHING IN fantasy novels, characters are everything in all the novels. If your characters aren't dynamic, interesting, complex, and compelling, then you can't expect the reader to care about them. And if the reader doesn't care about them, it's going to be hard to get them to keep reading your book. And the purpose of a book is to be read. Writing is a collaboration with the reader; if a book is never read, then it is never truly finished.

Give the reader characters to care about. They don't have to like them, but they do need to care.

Plot

Hopefully, something happens in your book. You can create the most amazing world ever and populate it with complicated and sympathetic characters, but if all they do is sit around the dinner table chatting, it might not be that great a read. So create a conflict, ask a question, make them uncomfortable. Remember, it's a dangerous business stepping out your front door; give them a push if you need to, but get them out that door.

Theme

If these four elements are vowels, than theme is the Y. I tend to not think about theme until my first draft is done. Until then, I don't really know what the book is about in the larger sense. But I also know a number of writers who use theme as their jumping off point. "I want to explore the politics of addiction" or "I want to write about racism and how it is exacerbated by class structures." Fantasy is an excellent genre for exploring very thorny issues at a bit of a remove.

DON'T WORRY IF YOU ONLY have one of these elements figured out, or if "figured out" is massively overstating how much you know about the project you're starting. Any of the four elements can grow organically out of the others, and even if you only have a tiny piece of one element, a lot can grow from that. In the next segment, I'll talk about a story coming out in an anthology soon that began with me thinking, "I'd like to set a story in the trenches of WWI."

That was it. That was all I had to start. Everything else grew organically out of that germ of an idea of a setting. No matter how slim a sliver of an idea you have, you can begin with it.

Starting with a Setting: The World-Building Approach

SETTING TOPS THIS LIST, AS IT is a uniquely fantasy starting point. No one starts a literary novel by saying, "I will set this in a world exactly like…this world." Yes, I'm over-simplifying and setting is important in every genre of novel, but I refuse to let the opportunity for a cheap laugh go by.

What if?
So, how to start? Fantasy is the literature of "What if?" (Science Fiction is, as well, which is why they are always linked. But the answers that genre comes up with are

different than ours.) Whenever you find yourself stuck, ask yourself "What if?" and let your mind go. It can be difficult for setting, as it is a question more suited to plot, but it still works. Some what ifs I've used to get started:

- What if Edinburgh was home to the Faery Market?
- What if Tsar Nicholas II had dragons?
- What if Scandinavia was much closer to the Levant?

All of these questions led me to know exactly where and when my stories would happen: Edinburgh, modern day; Russia at the onset of the Russian Revolution; a secondary world with cultures approximating Viking Age and early Levant peoples. At that point, I begin research to flesh out my knowledge of these settings. Often in researching the setting, I will discover my plot and characters.

Just Pick One

Just pick one. I have at least one novel and one novelette where I started with only the settings. For the first, I was walking through the tunnels of Abbot/Northwestern Hospital that allow you to travel for blocks through the giant complex without going outside in the cold Minnesota winters when I thought, "What a great setting for a zombie apocalypse."

For the novelette, I wanted to set a dark fantasy/horror in the trenches in WWI. I wrote about a thousand words to start, and decided I liked it enough to continue. At that point, I started researching WWI trench warfare. As often happens in these situations, I discovered that what I'd written so far was incompatible with the truth of the setting I'd chosen. I threw it away and began again. This is not uncommon. Don't get so stuck on something—whether idea, plot, character, etc.—that you can't adjust it to accommodate new knowledge. That new information invariably improves your story, even if it means deleting some work. I once deleted nine pages of a novel because I realized my character had been acting like someone else during that stretch. It was either rewrite those nine pages or rewrite the entire character. He was the main character and I was about 30,000 words in. It was an easy choice.

After I rewrote my beginning to the WWI story, I dove back into research. Again, I discovered that what I'd written wasn't going to work. It didn't matter, as I'd discovered some amazing facts. One, that there were legends about flesh-eating ghouls living in the No Man's Land between the trenches. And two, that there were medieval stone tunnels beneath Germany and France that no one knew the purpose of, and that one of them was called The Goblin Hole. At that point, the story nearly wrote itself.

This is not an uncommon occurrence with any of these starting points: when you decide on one and begin increasing your knowledge about it, the other pieces fall into place. So if you see a cool spot in your travels—real or imagined—that might be all you need to get started.

World-Building

You're going to need to do this at some point, so why not start with it? Personally, I love world-building. I draw maps, write histories, theologies, legends and rumors—anything that deepens my understanding of the world my characters are moving through. The important part to remember about world-building is to use Hemingway's

Iceberg Principle. Hemingway said that "The dignity of movement of an ice-berg is due to only one-eighth of it being above water." Always show less than you know. And never more than your POV characters know. But at the start of the process, build as much of the world as possible.

There are many methods of world-building, but they can usually be broken down into three distinct categories. But none are exclusive, and the best worlds use parts of all three to complete the process.

The Scientific Approach

This approach makes the most sense and is the one I use least often, as I am not a scientist. However, I like to know enough so that when I create my fantastical setting, I don't have to complete break physics to do so. Or if I do, I know where I have to use magic to set it right again. It can also lead to some interesting considerations, even in a magical environment: what happens to the excess mass when someone shape-shifts into a smaller creature? How does the action/reaction dynamic work with spellcasting? Is dragon fire a chemical reaction or a magical one? All of these scientific questions can lead you to some interesting places.

Where I like to use the scientific approach is in the smaller details. I want my wounds to be real. I want my horses to act like horses. I want my meals prepared in a way appropriate to the technology of the time. I want my weapons, armor, and tactics to make sense. In some ways, getting these details right is even more important than the broad swaths of world-building. Readers will often accept a wild concept to jump into a book, but if the details throw them right back out, then it's over.

The Historical Approach

A working knowledge of history is probably the most useful tool a fantasy writer can have. There is so much weird and wonderful in the history of this world that it takes very little to draw from that and turn it into fantasy. George R. R. Martin did this to great effect in his *Game of Thrones*, modeling the many different cultures in his world off of historical examples. You do want to file the serial numbers off, however. A historical people is a nice start, but you must make it your own—unless, you're doing historical fantasy, of course. Jane Yolen and I did that in *The Last Tsar's Dragons* when we took the Russian Revolution and made just one change: added dragons to it.

For my latest book, *Duster*, I have an 1800 year timeline of the land's history, with important dates and personages noted. Using the iceberg principle, much of this history is unmentioned by any characters, but most of them know it, or have an inkling of their home's history. It informs their own lives and history, even if they never make mention of it. And it makes them more real for it.

The Religious/Magical Approach

My absolute favorite thing to do is write the myths my characters believe. How the world was born. How humans and whatever magical beings inhabit my worlds were created. And since I'm writing fantasy, these legends can be as real as I want them to be. In *Duster*, the myths are real enough that they have repercussions for the plot and the characters. In my current work, *Deed of Empire*, there's no magic, but there's plenty of religion. And if the characters believe, than I need to be detailed in what they believe in. I've written several myths, some of which have made it into the text of the book, and I have a grid with all the gods from the different pantheons that I've come up with so far. In many fantasies, the tale of how the god or gods created the world is the exact truth of how it happened. It's fantasy. Go wild.

Starting with a Character(s)

SOMETIMES YOU DON'T KNOW where your story takes place or what's going to happen, but you know who it's about. This can be a hard place to start, but it can have very satisfying conclusions as a connection to the characters is essential. If the reader doesn't connect with the characters in a book, it's unlikely they'll respond to anything else.

There's a lot of information out there on questions to ask your characters, interview questions to help you understand them better. I don't tend to use them, but they are a useful tool, and when starting with just a character it's useful to know as much about this character as you can. Because by the end, you'd better know everything about them to make them real to the reader. Not show all of it, of course, but knowledge of their history, their loves and hates, their goals and dreams, will give an internal consistency to their actions that you can't replicate just by having them walk robot-like through the designated plot. If a character needs to change their core behavior to fit the plot, then either the plot needs altering or you need to rework the character from the inside out so that their actions are compatible with their inner workings.

Starting with a character is great in conjunction with a setting that is alien to them. Fish out of water stories carry within them a natural conflict that leads easily to plot. Also, having a viewpoint character who is unfamiliar with the setting allows you to be more descriptive and inquisitive about the setting, and allows for a "reader insert" into the tale. The reader can experience the unknown world along with the character.

Starting with a Plot

THIS IS BY FAR THE MOST common way for people to approach beginning a book, so why have I listed it third in a four point list? Because, for me, the plot must always be subservient to the characters. Nothing drives me crazier than seeing characters act oddly simply so the plot can go where the author needs it to go.

Don't do this.

However, knowing the basics or in the case of very detailed outliners, everything, about the plot of your book can make the writing of it very easy. For others, it takes the impetus of writing away; they already know what happens, so there's no joy of discovery while writing.

When I start with a plot, it's usually in the form of a beginning and an end point. The middle is quite vague. This allows me the best of both worlds: I have a beginning and something to aim for, but will still be surprised by what happens in the middle. Additionally, each time I've begun this way, when I reached my envisioned end point, I realized the book was not done and continued on past it.

If you do start with a plot, understand that that is all you're doing: *starting* with it. As you learn more about the characters, setting, and theme of the story you're telling, the plot will likely change, sometimes in small ways, sometimes large. If you allow it to, the book will likely improve because of it. If you force the other three elements to conform to the strictures of the plot you envisioned at the beginning of the process, you can end up with something lifeless and bland.

Again, this notion is not shared by all authors. A writer I deeply respect once said, "Words are my tools and I am the carpenter. They can no more change on their own than a hammer can." They outline their work extensively and then write it, claiming it comes out exactly as they envisioned it every time. I deem it likely that the moments of surprise, growth, and unexpected shifts all simply get moved to the detailed outlining process.

Regardless, whether you're outlining or flying by the seat of your pants, make sure your characters are true to their internal motivations as they move through the plot you've designed.

Starting with a Theme

TO BE HONEST, I'VE NEVER had a theme in mind when starting a book. I usually discover it partway through the rewrites and let it inform my edits. For instance, it was only when editing *Singer of Souls* did I discover that the book was about addiction. That thought had never crossed my mind during the first draft. My main character being a junkie was just an interesting way for him to ingest the magic that enabled him to see into the Faery realm. But as I wrote, I was true to the character as a junkie, and it affected his decision-making. The tale grew darker and ended badly, as most junkies' tales do.

Starting with a theme is difficult. With any of the other three elements you can start writing immediately, describing your setting or your character or simply setting your plot in motion. With a theme, you're usually going to need to add at least one of the other elements to the mix before you actually get down to putting words on paper.

Putting it All Together

As I said at the start of the chapter, when you say you have an idea for a book, you generally mean you have one or more of these elements in mind. Here's how I've started some of my books.

Singer of Souls

For this one, I had the setting first. In Edinburgh during the Fringe Festival, on the walk from Waverly Station to High Street there used to be a casual open air market that did business on the walkway that runs past the National Museum. The interesting thing (to me) was that despite there being two sides to the walkway, the merchants only set up on one side. The question was, "Why?" There were reasonable reasons, like zoning laws or crowd control or maybe the left side was public property but the right belonged to the museum. But to me, the fantasist, the answer was obvious: because that's where the Faery Market set up. In fact, the Faery Market had been there longer than the festival had. The Festival had grown up around the Market, drawn by the magic, despite humans being unable to see it.

So, there was my setting. I dove in, describing Edinburgh at the height of the Fringe, which is phantasmagoric enough all by itself. Adding the Faery Market was just icing on the cake. My viewpoint character was a man who already had the ability to see the market, an experienced practitioner of arcane arts who had symbols of power hennaed onto his hands to keep him safe from the often malicious fey.

If you've read the book, you know that neither that character nor the henna mechanic made it into the final version of the book. But it didn't matter, I'd begun. And after a few false starts, instead of master wizard I'd started with, I settled on Douglas, the junkie busker who was ill-equipped for what was coming his way.

The Hostage Prince

This trilogy, written with Jane Yolen (my mother), came from my idea for a character, but involved a little bit of history and Faery lore, as well. From my research for *Singer of Souls,* I knew a great deal about the legends of the Seelie and Unseelie Courts that were in constant opposition in the land of the fey. Coupled with the historical custom of sending noble sons to enemy kingdoms to ensure peace, I decided it would be fun to tell the story of a Seelie Prince raised in Unseelie lands. Since my mother is an avowed "pantser" there was never any talk of developing the plot more than that before we got started. She added Snail, the brave midwife's apprentice, and off we went.

Duster

This one also began with a character, but is really an example of using all four elements to get a story rolling.

I was kind of stuck one morning, sitting at my computer with no active projects. On a whim, I decided to pull a character out of the back corner of my mind where he'd been sitting for over a decade: a rough piece of business, half elf/half human and an outcast from both worlds. He has the words "Half Breed" tattooed across his knuckles.

Strangely, instead of writing from this character's viewpoint, my first view of him was from another character's first person POV, looking down the length of a sword that the half-elf held at his throat. Also, the character was now half-human and half something else. Some kind of sentient feline creature.

What the hell?

But, hey, these things happen. I extricated my main character from danger and my half-breed stomped off in a huff, probably because he wasn't the main character. But suddenly, I'm left in the head of a person I hadn't planned for. That's all right, I brought his family in for breakfast and learned more about them. Also, one of his sons was missing.

Aha! I thought, sensing the telltale sign of a plot developing. *The game is afoot.*

I made the missing son a middle son and an addict, though the drugs were a bit different this world. "Write what you know" is not as difficult as you think, even in a fantasy setting. Guess who was a troubled middle child who battled addiction until well into his thirties?

I spent a couple of chapters with my main character, now an old, fat tavernkeeper who twenty years ago was once an elite soldier. Unfortunately, he doesn't know where his son is or why he's missing or why the half-breed was looking for him. (Oh yeah, I added that.) Even more unfortunately, neither did I.

At this point, I realized I was wandering around in a setting I didn't know nearly enough about. I had a bunch of characters I thought were interesting and some enticing hints at a plot (I was especially fond of the dynamic between Mika and his old army buddy, Gair, who was a murderous pimp and generally heinous individual, but absolutely loyal to Mika) but I needed to know more about the world before I could decide what was happening.

When you run into problems with your manuscript, often the best thing to do is to try to write your way through them. Nothing is lost and you can always go back and fix it when you edit. But remember, when you write through it, it doesn't necessarily have to be in the manuscript itself.

I wrote the creation myth of the world.

This was not an accident. When I study settings for historical fiction (I've had three straight up historical stories published as well as an historical fantasy novella) I don't just study the time period I'll be writing in. That would give me only a very surface idea of the place and people. I study the history of what led up to it, as well as the myths and monsters the cultures within believe now and believed way back when. Sometimes, when writing fantasy, the history of the religions and folktales of a region are more important than the true history of the place. You should know them both, but I especially concentrate on the myth-making a culture partakes in.

Now that I was creating an entire world of my own, I realized I was going to need to know their creation myths if I were to know the peoples. So I wrote it. I actually never intended it to go in the book. I wrote it solely for my own edification and to understand the world I was creating. But as happens sometimes, I got more than I'd expected. When I was done with the creation myth, I had added two more races to the mix and come up with a plot.

. . .

Deed of Empire

This book's beginning was entirely world-building. Before I put a single sentence on my screen, I designed an entire world and its history. I had kept the world of *Duster* intentionally small with unnavigable nightly tides around an island nation, but this time I wanted to spread out into a much wider and much more complex world. I drew a map, then placed cultures on it. I envisioned how they would have interacted with each other over the centuries to end up where they were. I invented some cultures that had been wiped out by the current ones. Added some even more ancient ones that had only left ruins. Peoples moved and split from their parent cultures but still retained similar languages/gods/customs. Rivalries built on centuries of invasion and counter-invasion developed between neighbors. Empires took over wide swaths of land then declined, leaving imprints of their culture on the conquered. I added a Silk Road-type trade network that connected far flung empires and placed a giant city-state at the crossroads, a hub of mercantile activity.

I had a lot of fun.

Then I dropped four characters into four different countries and let them explore the world. After a few chapters and a couple of rewrites of those chapters, I'd winnowed it down to three POV characters and not only had the bones of a plot for this book, I had the arc for the next two books in what is now a trilogy.

3
POINT OF VIEW

Point of view is the eye that opens into the world you're creating. It is of utmost importance. As a writer friend once said, "If you think point of view is unimportant, try looking at your own ear."

There are two decisions to be made regarding point of view. You must decide what point of view you're going to write in, and you must decide who your point of view character(s) will be.

First, Second, and Third Person Point of View

THERE ARE ONLY THREE POINTS of view, but there are a few subsets of them with important differences. And matched with tense—past or present, mostly—you have a lot of choices to pick from. All are valid, but they all also come with strengths and weaknesses. Picking the correct viewpoint for your story is essential, though you can go back and switch it if it's not working. It's not an enjoyable task if you've already written a great deal but it can be done. So don't despair if you've started in one and need to switch to another.

First Person — The "I" point of view:

I swung my sword. I hit the troll. He laughed and crushed my skull.

Strengths:

- Biggest emotional impact
- Action is immediate and visceral
- Have access to all the main character's thoughts and feelings

Weaknesses:

- Knowledge of the world is limited to what the viewpoint character knows
- Scope of the story is limited to what the viewpoint character experiences
- Can be difficult to create true concern in the reader for the POV character, as they are presumably telling the story

First person point of view is a great POV for a first novel. The limits work in your favor, as you aren't overwhelming yourself or the reader with extraneous information about the world. One of the traps fantasy writers fall into is being so excited about the inner workings of the world they've created that they want to tell the reader all about it. In detail. Enormous, exasperating detail. These "info dumps" or "expository lumps" are a death knell for reader engagement, as very few readers are as excited about the world on its own as the author is. They grow excited about the world by watching the characters move through it and experience it.

First person, when done correctly, self-corrects those problems. You can only describe what your one character is seeing and doing, you can only tell the reader what that one character knows. Unless that character is an historian scientist adventurer general, it's going to be hard to get lost in descriptive sidetracks about the world.

(Ed. Note: There is now an 85% chance that Adam's next book will have an historian scientist adventurer general in it)

It is an intuitive, story-telling way to write, and it is very easy to develop a voice in first-person because you are always writing in character.

Second Person — The "You" point of view

You swung your sword. You hit the troll. He laughed and crushed your skull.

Strengths:

- Artistic and Unique

Weaknesses:

- Difficult to write in
- Off-putting to most readers

- Extremely difficult to carry through an entire novel

I would not suggest you try to write a novel in second person without a very compelling reason to do so. Though it should be the most immediate and visceral—you are literally telling the reader what they're experiencing—the actual effect is nothing like that. In novels, I have seen it used effectively in interstitial pieces and intros, but I doubt its ability to carry through an entire book.

Third Person — The "He/She/They" point of view

She swung her sword. She hit the troll. He laughed and crushed her skull.

Strengths:

- Can have as many viewpoint characters as necessary to tell the story
- Unlimited world detail available

Weaknesses:

- Emotional impact can be lessened
- Action can be at a remove, less visceral

Third person is a great point of view for those great, sweeping epics that are difficult to tell through only one set of eyes. If your novel spans the nations/planes/realms you may need this viewpoint to tell it. The danger is that by spreading out your tale as well as telling it from outside your characters' heads, the emotional impact of their own story gets watered down to the point that the reader no longer cares what happens to them. However, Third Person Limited, a subset of third person, can help with this.

Tenses, Subsets, and Combinations

THERE ARE TWO USEFUL TENSES: past and present. Future tense, like second person, can hold through some specialty sections if your story needs it, but I doubt its ability to carry through a whole novel. You may certainly attempt a second person novel in future tense, but I have nothing useful to tell you by way of instruction for it. Past and present tense translate easily into *I did* or *I do*. Or to use my sample sentence:

I swung my sword. (First person, past tense)

They swing their sword. (Third person, present tense)

The strengths and weaknesses of the two tenses are fairly obvious: past tense is less immediate, but is a very natural way to tell a story. Present tense is *very* immediate, but it can be a strain to carry through a novel—for me. For several writers in my writers group, present tense is their natural tense, and they write most of their material in it. As a reader, I find that if a story is in past tense, I fall right into it, but if it is in present tense, I notice it for a bit. But not long. A page or two and I'm in it. So past or present tense can be a largely personal choice on the surface, but when combined with point of view—and some specific subsets of those points of view—you end up with a great deal of choices for how to write your novel.

. . .

First Person, Present Tense

Without a doubt, the most present and visceral POV. Common in YA and middle-grade fantasy as it's a real attention grabber and younger readers often need that to get drawn in. If you want a fantasy that is eyes-on and locked in, with one character driving all the action, this is the tense for you. Great for urban fantasy as you don't have to explain any of the workings of the real world to the reader. And when you get to the eldritch part, it is usually all new to the main character, so describing it isn't rehashing material the character already knows.

I haven't written a novel-length piece in this POV, but I've done a number of stories in it. I really like the drive of this tense for shorter works.

First Person, Past Tense

In theory, this POV could be slightly less visceral than the present tense version, but in practice they're nearly identical. The slight remove of past tense versus present is balanced by the naturalness of the combination for telling a story.

I find both first person tenses are excellent for stories where the fantasy element isn't present at the start of the book and you can experience the wonder from inside the character's head as they discover it.

Third Person Omnipotent, Past Tense

This is the classic epic fantasy point of view, where the narrator is omnipotent and can jump inside any character's head at any time, told in the past tense. It is considered quite archaic these days. Readers expect far more emotional impact from their books than the era when this

POV was popular. Using the omnipotent POV in present tense is not likely to help with the problems it suffers from. However, as a specialty POV—in a throwback or experimental piece, perhaps—it might have some potential. But you must be very aware of the "rules" you'd be breaking using it. Those rules are set out next in the very popular and useful, third person limited.

Third Person Limited, Past Tense

This POV has far surpassed omnipotent in popularity and, to my mind, utility. In third person limited, you can have any amount of viewpoint characters you want, but when you write a scene, you stay inside only one character's head. This gives you an approximation of a first person POV's immediacy and intimacy, while still allowing you the freedom and scope of third person. You still have to only reveal the parts of the world or plot that the current POV character knows, but given enough POV characters, there's no reason you can't reveal all you need to without resorting to the dreaded expository lumps. The thing to avoid is "head-hopping," jumping from one character's inner thoughts to another's within a single scene. Keep to one character per scene/chapter and this can be a great POV.

Third Person Limited, Present Tense

Subjectively, this POV has a feel to it that is more literary than fantasy. In fact, one of my two non-genre sales uses it. But again, this is entirely subjective, and there's no reason it wouldn't work in a fantasy setting. But third person limited past tense is by far the more common tense. If "invisible prose" is your aim—writing in such a way that the language doesn't distract or interfere with the story—then past tense would be the preferred tense. However, the little added drive from being in present tense might be just the thing to kick your tale into overdrive.

Combinations

I have seen all of these POVs work in combination with one another and have combined them myself:

- *Duster* is written in first person past tense, but has a great number of interstitial scenes thrown in with varying points of view and tenses, as well as a third-person limited, past tense narrative that joins in the second half of the book.
- In *The Last Tsar's Dragons,* the only non-historical character is an unnamed functionary written in first person, present tense for the first and last chapters and past tense for the remainder. The rest of the characters are in third person limited past tense.
- Jonathan Maberry's *Joe Ledger Series* uses a similar pattern. Ledger's first person narrative is interspersed with third person limited chapters of a wide variety of characters, often the main antagonists. It really ramps up the drama to know more of what horrible things are coming than the hero does.
- A writer in my group wrote a novel with three first person, present tense narratives in it. It was initially a tough read, but they put a lot of work into making the three different voices very

distinct, and it ended up being an absolutely rollicking ride.

These are just a few combinations that come to mind. Don't be afraid to add points of view or change the one you started with to better serve the story you're trying to tell.

Point of View Characters

If I have one hard and fast rule for all of writing, it is this: your protagonist must have an effect on the denouement of the story. With multiple points of view, you have a lot more room to maneuver. But especially in first person, or third person tight (which is just third person limited with only one POV character) it is essential that your character affect the action. If not, then why didn't you tell the story of someone who did? I once read a fantasy novel that could have been brilliant, but the main character turned out to only be an observer in the final, climactic events. It was disheartening to invest that much time in a novel and be let down at the end.

This is not to say that your protagonist has to win, or even survive. But they must drive the action in some way, or it's likely the reader would prefer the story be from the viewpoint of someone who did. There's a reason there's so many stories about kings and queens: they are at the head of huge events. I like the story of the apprentice pig-minder who becomes a hero even more, because it's the tale of someone who has no expectation of driving events, but ends up doing so.

That's not to say that you can't write a small story. Small stakes can be just as dramatic as big ones. But again, if the POV character doesn't have some affect on the events, then why are you telling their story?

Putting it Together

MY SUGGESTIONS FOR viewpoints given your choice from the four elements:

Starting with a Setting:

If your setting is a big secondary world, I'd suggest third person limited, past tense. It gives you the freedom to jump around and explore the world and find the story within it. Pick characters from different social strata, different locales, different cultures. Don't worry about whether they have any place in your story. You can always cut them out if they don't, but will have learned about your world in the process. For *Deed of Empire*, I started with a young thief, an old raider chief, a puppet empress, and a young mercenary newly promoted to a leadership position. At the time, I had no idea how their tales would intersect; that developed as I wrote. One character—the puppet empress—I cut out of this book and moved to the sequel. It was unpleasant to take three finished chapters out of my draft, but now that it's finished, I get paid on the backend: I already have three chapters of the sequel written.

If your setting is smaller and more contained, first person or a tight third person limited can be good. But these tight POVs lend themselves to more plot-oriented stories, so you have less time to wander around trying to find one. But writing is a forgiving medium, because up until its published, you can always go back and make it look like you wrote it that way the first time. For *Pay the Piper*, our original idea was to write a rock and roll vampire tale. There are zero vampires in it.

Starting with a Character

This should be straightforward: More than one character? Third person limited, past tense. Just the one? First person. Past or present, depending on personal preference. Lean toward present if its YA or middle-grade.

However, as illustrated by how I began *Duster*, starting with a character doesn't mean that they're automatically your viewpoint character. Don't be afraid to switch to a different character if you start feeling like the character you began the story with isn't going to play that big a role in the story. Once again, there are zero vampires in *Pay the Piper*. And it won an award.

Starting with a Plot

If it's a multi-threaded, world-spanning plot, lean toward third person limited. You'll probably need more than one character to tell it. But if the plot is about a multi-threaded, world-spanning conspiracy that will be brought down by one intrepid hero, then first person is definitely in the running.

Consider whether your plot is intrigue or action, complex or direct. Complex is different than a surprise twist. Complex is often better served in third person limited; surprise twists work great in first person where the reader experiences the shock of the twist right along with the protagonist.

Go back and look at the strengths and weaknesses of the points of view. What do you want to emphasize? The beauty of the surroundings? The complexity of the plot? Or do you want pure visceral impact and excitement? Answer those questions and the POV will suggest itself to you.

For the viewpoint character, you need to look at your plot and decide who drives most of the action. That's the one.

Starting with a Theme

Sky's kind of the limit with this one, as the concept of the novel is probably quite vague at this point. However, consider whether the theme you want to explore is a deeply personal one or of a more universal nature. It's not a coincidence that my books that explore addiction are all in first person and the ones that consider the politics of power are mostly in third.

4

STRUCTURE

So, you've got an idea for a book, you've decided on a point of view and a viewpoint character, and you've begun to write. And now you're thinking about structure.

My advice? Don't.

Though there are some writers who begin with a structure and go from there, I like to let the structure of the book grow out of the writing itself. Because if it doesn't serve the story, then why is it there?

I learned this, of course, by writing.

I had just begun working on *Singer of Souls,* my first solo novel, and the second novel that I'd ever written. Or the first and a half depending on how you count writing *Pay the Piper* with a co-author. After a few false starts, I'd settled on my main character, Douglas, the drug-addicted busker; my setting, Edinburgh and the Faery Market; and I had a bit of a plot, as I had an ending scene in mind: Douglas, guitar in hand, walking into Faery which he knew was the only place where he'd have the power to defeat Aine, the Queen of Faery.

Unfortunately, I also had a structure in mind. I explained it to my mother on the phone.

"I begin with Douglas at the Faery Market. He can already see the fey. I'll go forward from there as the plot develops while telling the backstory—how he ended up in Edinburgh, how he gained the ability to see into the Faery world, etc.—in alternating chapters."

I'd called her, because after four chapters, I'd become completely stuck and could see no way forward.

She listened patiently to all my plans for the novel, and in guru-like fashion, told me, "Why don't you start at the beginning and tell it through to the end?"

I threw away my overcomplicated and unnecessary structure and I was never blocked again on that book.

Additionally, she explained another reason not to do the flashback. The moment that Douglas first discovers that he can see the fey is the defining moment of his life. If I tell it at a remove, I lose a lot of the emotional impact of the scene. As a beginning writer, I realized that I was a little afraid of not being good enough to write the scene the way it needed to be written. But good or not, I had to be brave and attempt it, or there was no sense writing the novel at all.

In other books, I have used very complicated structures. But they grew out of the story and helped to move things along.

Duster opens with the myth of how the three races of the land were born and then dives into Mika's first person narrative. It seems a throw away, merely a way to introduce the reader to the world they're entering. But if that was it's only purpose, I never would've opened with it. It's nearly always better to let the reader experience the world through the eyes of the viewpoint character(s). However, as the story goes on, it's revealed that the creation myth is key to the plot. Furthermore, by that point there have been more excerpts of creation myth, some from the POV of the other races. And they tell a very different story from the human one. And through those readings, though the action to this point has been if not benevolent, not particularly devastating to the characters, the reader gets the sinking feeling that dark and powerful forces are moving behind the scenes and there will soon be terrible consequences for the heroes. This ramped up the tension nicely, without having to add anything artificial to the main first-person narrative. While in Mika's head, we only know what he knows, but I add to that with these "historical" documents in the interstitial sections.

In addition to those pieces, Mika's story includes flashbacks every third chapter to his time in the army twenty years ago. This is a bit different than Douglas's flashback. Though there are some defining moments in Mika's background, they only make sense with what is happening in the now—and what is happening in the now is being revealed as so much bigger than anything in his past.

As a side note, one of my favorite things about Mika recounting his time in the army that I'm not sure anyone has truly caught. If readers pay attention to the way other characters react to meeting him when he's older, a savvy reader will realize that he downplays his actions during the war quite a bit. As opposed to being in the right place at the right time a couple of times and looking heroic largely because Gair was with him and killed a bunch of enemies, Mika is the hero of a ton battles and is an absolute legend to anyone who fought in the Second Duster War.

But I digress, because the structure isn't even done yet. Mika's two timelines meet in the middle of the book. In the first draft of the story, I just went on, though the lack of those every third chapter time shifts made it a bit wonky.

But as I had nothing to put there, I didn't think there was much to do. However, my writers group pointed out (rightly) that I had given Mika's wife, Jehanna—who was as magical and destined as him in her own way—very short shrift after she was kidnapped. She just disappeared until the very end, where she does do something magical to help, but it's not huge and is pretty lost in all the chaos of the climax.

Well, there was my answer to the wonkiness of losing the flashback chapters. When Mika's narrative combined into one, I added a third-person narrative of Jehanna to replace it. And following my rules of viewpoint characters —which she now was—instead of providing a little help at the end, her actions are the sole reason Mika is able to continue on and save the day.

If I tried to describe this structure plainly, it would make no sense at all. And there is no chance I would have come up with it beforehand. But as it grew organically through the writing of the book, and every piece of it served the story, it flows quite naturally.

Like every other "rule" in this book, if you like to start with a structure, go for it. I have a writer friend who doesn't write anything until he has a structure for it. And if the story doesn't suit the structure, he throws the story out, which is anathema to my way of thinking. However, he has written both brilliant and best-selling books, so obviously, it works for him. It's how *he* writes.

But my general rule is, absent a compelling reason to do otherwise, that a story is best begun at the beginning and told through to the end.

5

PANTSERS VS. PLOTTERS

In recent years, it has become popular for writers to define themselves as "Pantsers"—writers who 'fly by the seat of their pants'—or "Plotters"—those who plot everything beforehand. These are fun terms, and are useful as general guidelines if you're trying to define your preferred method of working. But I've yet to meet a writer who's a pure version of either. Every Pantser I know spends a little bit of time planning out some plot points; every Plotter has sailed off into the void at some time with no idea where they're going to land. To me, the main difference seems to be in *when* they do it.

Pantsers tend to go a long ways into a book before finally deciding to sit down and figure out what the hell is going on. Plotters often find an unnoticed gap in the dreaded middle of a work that they need to fill and send their characters off without a map to fill it.

As I think you can tell from this book, I wouldn't call myself either one. I've written books in both ways. *Singer of Souls* was very much a plotted book, with a fairly detailed synopsis. But even in that, I had a very "Panster" moment near the end.

I needed one last scene with Douglas and his sort-of girlfriend, Sandy. A final goodbye to his last vestiges of humanity. I didn't quite know what was going to happen in that scene, but I sent him up the stairs to her apartment. She let him in, and then the door closed behind him. Turning around, there were two other rough-looking characters in there with her. I suddenly realized that things had changed quite a bit for Douglas, and that far from being a quick goodbye and on to the next section of the plot, he was in a great deal of trouble. I wasn't sure if he was going to survive the encounter. As he was my main character, his death would throw a real wrench into my story and I'd need to rewrite the scene. But I kept writing, waiting to see if Douglas could extricate himself from what had a become a dangerous situation. He survive the encounter—while acting in character—and in the end, what was going to be a needed, but kind of throwaway scene, became defining of the trouble he'd put himself in, as well as signaling the beginning of the spiraling descent that was the climax of the book.

Duster was pantsed for much of it, from its start as just a single character, to Mika's travels into the Duster homelands and the Galloch underworld. I had no idea what was going to happen in those places. Even when I wrote the creation myth and discovered a plot, what I'd really figured out was who the players were and what each side was trying to accomplish. I had no idea what was going to happen. I certainly had no idea how Mika was going to be able to stop it. And since I'm not averse to writing tragedy, I wasn't certain he was going to.

If the author is worried about how things are going to end, think how the reader feels.

So, whether you think you're a pantser or a plotter, you'll probably need a little of both to finish a novel.

6

TIPS AND TRICKS

Writing fantasy presents unique challenges that need unique skills to overcome. Here are a few tips and tricks to get you started:

World-building — Make sure your world-building is helping you begin, not keeping you from it. If you haven't started writing because you feel like you haven't fleshed the world out enough yet, just begin anyway. Even the world-building is subordinate to the story. I've had to change something in the history/architecture/ecology of every world I've built due to the story heading off in a different direction. Let it, and then mold the world to fit the new path. You can flesh out the world to fit the story you want to tell at any time in the process. The reader won't know.

The other world-building problem is throwing everything you know about the world into the book, completely breaking the iceberg principle. If you find yourself doing this, don't worry. You'll fix it in the rewrites. Go ahead and let your excitement drive you, if that's what it takes to start and maintain momentum.

Ekphrasis — Yeah, that's a word: a literary description of or commentary on a visual work of art. I know I said the ideas are the easy part, but that's not always true. If you're feeling stuck, try ekphrasis as a way to jumpstart your brain. There's all kinds of fantasy phrases you can follow on Pinterest or similar sites to look at art that can spark the creative synapses in your brain. Find a piece and start writing about it. You never know what's going to happen once you start writing.

And understand, ekphrastic rummaging, online research, interviewing experts, reading, and any number of other activities are all part of the writing process. You are not wasting time with these activities. Not every moment of every day can be spent at the keyboard pecking away like a coked up corvid. Sometimes you need to sit quietly and allow your thoughts space and time to germinate.

What if? — Let's talk a little more about "what if?" It is truly the most powerful question in the fantasist's lexicon. But it can also be a broad and rather daunting place to begin. Instead of starting brand new, try your hand at these popular what ifs:

- *The POV Shift* — What if a well-known myth or tale was told from a different character's viewpoint. Gregory Maguire has mined this for very good effect. And don't limit yourself to the obvious. My mother once rewrote Billy Goat's Gruff from the viewpoint of the bridge; there really is no limit to what can be attempted.
- *Modernization* — Bring the mythic into the modern world—that's pretty much Urban Fantasy right there. Take a tale or character

from myth or lore and put them in the modern world. Or do it in reverse, and place your modern character into the ancient or mythical world.
- *Believing is Seeing* — Take any myth, legend, superstition, magic, folk belief and make it real. Lots of fun to be had with this, whether set in historical, modern times, or a secondary world of your own devising.

7

TRAPS, PITFALLS, AND MISSTEPS

Here are some common mistakes first time fantasy writers make:

Smeerp — If it has long ears, a fluffy tail, eats carrots, and hops around, then call it a rabbit, not a *smeerp*. Any time there is an exact equivalent between a real world animal/plant/thing, just call it by its actual name. If the rabbit is carnivorous, then it gets a new name.

Names — Don't make up unpronounceable names. They're hard for the reader to keep track of, and the first time you do a live reading, you're going to regret the choice.

Character Knowledge — This is a tricky one. You have to balance what the reader needs to know vs. what the character sees as commonplace. For instance, you're not going to spend a lot of time describing how a window works. But if it's a magic window, you need to let the reader know. However, if all the windows in the world are magic and the viewpoint character sees them every day, there's no good reason for them to explain their function. It's a delicate balance and shows why a fish out of water main character who needs things explained to them is so popular in fantasy.

Expository Lumps — I covered this in the main text but it bears repeating: avoid long dumps of information. Consider:

- Does the viewpoint character have this information?
- Does the reader need this information?
- Is there any other way to elegantly get this information across? (Hint: there probably is)

And I caution you to especially avoid the long info dump at the very beginning of the book. Instead, begin with the story, and let the important details filter in as the story develops.

For instance:

The Kingdom of Rondan has been at war with its neighbor, Farrona, for a thousand years. Battles raged across the countryside, devastating the land. At a final battle, victory seems finally within reach, but both sides lose so many men, that as the survivors limp home, they worry that lawlessness and chaos will take over the land.

Gerrick was one of those soldiers.

We've got the gist of what's happening, but I'm already bored. How about this instead:

. . .

Gerrick lay in the mud and blood of the battlefield, left arm numb and trapped beneath his shattered shield. The hillside was littered with the dead, Rondan in blue, Farronian in red and gray. Gerrick wore the blue, though it was difficult to tell; his surcoat was so stained by battle and travel it appeared an unrecognizable brown.

Did we win? he thought, not bothering to say it aloud. There was no one alive to answer.

INSTEAD OF LAYING OUT THE background, I drop the reader right into the muddy, bloody world. I sneak in the two sides of the conflict and hint at the devastation. And I give the reader a character immediately. So instead of a distant view of a world they have no reason to care about, I show them the world through a character's eyes who has every reason to care as he lives there. Lead with character, with story. The other details will wait. Trust your reader to trust you and you'll both make it to the end of the book.

AFTERWORD

I hope this book has given you the tools you need to begin writing your fantasy novel. In the next book, *How to Write Fantasy Novels, Volume II: The First Draft*, I'll talk about all the tools you need to make it through your first draft and set yourself up for a good revision process.

For more writing tips, you can sign up for my newsletter at:

adamstemple.com/newsletter

or follow me on Facebook at facebook.com/adamstemple or Twitter @adamstemple4.

ALSO BY ADAM STEMPLE

HOW TO WRITE FANTASY NOVELS:
Volume I: Getting Started
Volume II: The First Draft
Volume III: Revising

OTHER BOOKS BY ADAM:
Bad Company
The Mika Bare-Hand Books
The Seelie Wars Trilogy

ABOUT THE AUTHOR

Adam Stemple is an award-winning author, poet, and musician. Of his first novel, SINGER OF SOULS, SFWA Grandmaster Anne McCaffrey said, "One of the best first novels I have ever read." Of his later works, Hugo Award winning author Naomi Kritzer said, "No one writes bastard-son-of-a-bitch characters as brilliantly as Adam Stemple."

Like most authors, his life experience is broad and odd. He spent twenty years on the road with a variety of bands playing for crowds of between 2 and 20,000 people. He started, ran, and sold a poker training site. He worked in a warehouse. He picked corn. He traded options and demoed houses. He drove pizzas for nine months in 1986, which for twenty-seven years was the longest he'd ever been employed. He drank too much and has now been sober for over fifteen years. He published his first book at the age of sixteen, "The Lullaby Songbook," which he arranged the music for. His mother is a famous children's book author. His children are artistic. His wife is a better person than him in nearly all regards.

WHERE TO FIND ADAM ONLINE

- www.adamstemple.com
- www.patreon.com/adamstemple
- www.facebook.com/adamstemple
- www.twitter.com/adamstemple4
- www.instagram.com/adamstemplebooks/
- www.amazon.com/author/adamstemple

Printed in Great Britain
by Amazon